Unveiled

A collection of short stories
portraying the hidden lives
of Indian women

VINITA SHAW

Copyright © 2013 by Vinita Shaw

All rights reserved. No part of this book may be used, reproduced, stored in a retrieval system, or transmitted in any form whatsoever — including electronic, photocopy, recording — without prior written permission from the author, except in the case of brief quotations embodied in critical articles or reviews.

Scripture quotations are taken from the *Holy Bible, New International Version*. NIV*. Copyright © 1973, 1978, 1984 by International Bible Society. Used by permission of Zondervan. All rights reserved.

The names have been changed to protect identity. The proceeds from the sale of *Unveiled* will go towards the work of Disha Foundation to help women and girls in India.

SECOND EDITION

ISBN: 978-1-939748-27-0

Disclaimer: The views and opinions expressed in this book are solely those of the author.

Printed by Vinita Shaw, Life Word Creations.
www.lifewordcreations.com

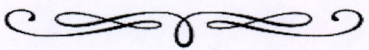

Jesus said,

"Woman, why are you crying?

Whom are you seeking?"

John 20:15

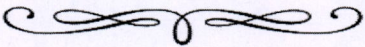

This book is dedicated to my father,

late Mr. John Missal

and

to my husband,

Pastor Timothy Shaw

Contents

Introduction 9
1. Womb or Tomb? 17
2. Trashed 23
3. Unsafe Haven 29
4. "Nakusha" – Unwanted 33
5. Vanished 37
6. Nipped in the Bud 43
7. Precious Girls 47
8. Goddess of Trash 51
9. Legacy of AIDS 55
10. Unwed Mother 59
11. Of Satan and Girls 65
12. Kidney For Sale 69
13. Much Ado About "I Do" 73
14. Happy Holidays 77
15. Torched Alive 85
16. Dared to Love 89
17. Living a Lie 95
18. "I Slipped" 97
19. Womb For Rent 101
20. Fired 105
21. "I Feel Dirty" 111
22. Abandoned 115
About the Author 119

INTRODUCTION

Having finished a workshop advocating gender equality from a Christian worldview at one of the elite schools in India, girls and boys lined up to meet our team when a 12-year-old girl kept badgering me with her volley of questions: "Why do they kill the girls in our country? Why are girls thrown in the trash? Why are people doing this to us? How come the majority of Indians worship goddesses and yet still kill the girl child?" She was so distraught that neither my words of consolation nor my comforting pat on her shoulder pacified her.

"*Why did you make me a girl?*" is a question I asked God early in life. From a tender age of ten, I had sensed something was not quite right with me. I'm the eldest of three girls born to Indian parents in New Delhi, the capital city of India. Living in a pluralistic society like India, comments like, "*Oh, you have three daughters, but no sons?*" were often flung at my parents in a plaintive tone with eyes filled with remorse. With the passage of time, these comments took their toll on me. I actually began to believe something was *definitely* wrong with me. I realized it was my gender – I was born a girl!

Smirks, ridicule and disrespect related to my gender became a way of life for me and developed within me a deep sense of inferiority complex which my education was not able to erase.

I was born into a culture where a newlywed woman is blessed with these words, *"May you be a mother of a thousand sons."*

For centuries, millions of Indians have believed that:
The way to heaven is through a son.
A thief has come when a daughter is born.
It is unlucky to have a daughter.
The first child must be a son.
A daughter is someone else's property.
A daughter is a burden on the father's head.

Casteism*, illiteracy, poverty and superstitious beliefs have further stroked this fire of gender disparity. To this day, in the majority of Indian homes, wailing, chest beating and gloom are the first welcome a girl receives from her own family, which view her as bad news. That is, if she is not terminated in the womb or choked to death shortly after birth.

If neither of the above happens, many girls suffer from systematic malnutrition, neglect, sexual abuse or are given into child marriage, offered as temple prostitutes, married to

---

* One of the hereditary social classes in Hinduism that restrict the occupation of their members and their association with the members of other castes.

many men in the same family due to a shortage of women, or burnt if they do not bring enough dowry. Still others are sold to feed the family, become victims of acid attacks and domestic violence, or are abandoned in their twilight years at religious gatherings, left to beg for a living.

But the mother of all tragedies is that the victim is often blamed for having invited her plight because of her gender – simply because she was born a girl.

Conditioned to believe that women are the second sex and hence inferior, objects of show only, their chastity is tied to the family honor. John Berger in his book, *Ways of Seeing*, says, *"From childhood, women's spaces are limited because they live under the tutelage of men. Slowly, women start surveying themselves in order to live up to the expectations of men. Gently persuaded, they are made to believe, feel, behave and act as inferior second-class citizens."*

As a miniscule percentage of girls begin to get educated, and against all odds press on toward economic independence, they are faced with the ire of the patriarchal system that feels power slip away from them.

With poor infrastructure in the villages and smaller cities of India, there is a big migrant population moving from the rural areas to the metro cities carrying with them their mindset against women. When they see educated and independent women, their hatred spills forth, sending the crime graph soar higher.

Further, she faces sexual harassment at the workplace and her husband's wrath at home. In the name of family honor, she tries her level best to salvage her marriage as she knows that social stigma will follow her single status since her true identity is always tied to her relation to a male member of her family.

The educated woman of today is beginning to react and break free, thereby sending the divorce rate spiraling upwards. The woman of today is very angry and no longer wishes to take it lying down. Armed with education and economic independence, she is on the warpath, with the collective anger of women spilling onto the streets in the form of protests and demonstration, ready to kill and die in the name of self-respect. Many have resorted to manipulation by making false allegations.

Even the educated Indian diaspora which migrates to other countries, carries with them their hatred for the girl child and in countries where Indian migrants reside in huge numbers, the gender ratio is skewed.

The government of India has made many robust laws that help women combat all these injustices. Yet, the laws are no more than paper tigers as those who implement them are usually men who believe that women are inferior, an object to be owned much akin to cattle.

It is not as if there are no Indian men who value women as their equal. Their numbers, however, are few for many are not able to stand against the tide and they buckle under societal pressures.

Gender experts believe that the challenges are immense, given the 1.2 billion plus population of India with its diversity and geographical spread. Education, along with vocational and financial training,they claim , is the tool that will play a major role in turning women from liability into asset.

However, this is not enough because, today, the gender related injustice and violence cuts across caste, class, education, region and religion.

I believe that only Christ has the power to transform mindsets that are rock hard.

In all the four Gospels, we find Christ interacting with men and women of all ages. His compassion and healing rose above gender, caste, creed and nationality.

With particular reference to women, Christ rose above the culture of His times to interact with them, doing so in a culture which is embodied in a Jewish man's prayer as he daily thanks God for not making him a Gentile, a dog or a woman.

It is Christ who came to the rescue of a woman in Mark 14:6. *"Leave her alone. Why are you bothering her?"*

It is Christ who asked Mary, *"Woman, why are you crying? Whom are you seeking?"* (John 20:15)

Christ did not degrade, ridicule, oppress, violate, isolate, devalue or patronize women. Instead, He recognized her as a human being and used her gift of influence, with the Samaritan woman who brought a village to faith in Him and with Mary of Magdala who became the first witness to His resurrection and told the disciples.

Christ came as the Saviour for men and women whom He loves and reaches out to equally.

Christ reinstated woman to the position that God had originally intended for her at the beginning of creation.

Dorothy Sayers put it very well when she wrote,

"Perhaps it is not a wonder that the women were first at the cradle and last at the cross. They had never known a man like this man – there never has been such another." (Taken from "Why Not Women" by Loren Cunnigham, YWAM publishing.)

The words of Christ have resonated and continue to do so through the centuries bringing healing, freedom from gender disparity, value, dignity, unconditional love, courage to stand up and the eternal hope of life to come. It is ours for the taking.

As Christ's representative, the Church has engaged and continues to engage with the context. However, it is not enough. The Church is further expected to pray for a transformation to take place and intervene to confront cultural beliefs which belie God's truth.

To borrow the words of Dr. John Stott who said, *"Proximity to and reverence for the Scriptures is not the same as obedience to it."*

The Church is expected to reach out to the wounded women as never done before and, like the Good Samaritan, "stop to render aid."

Further, it is also expected for the Church to rise above the local culture and release women for the work of the Great Commission for the Bible says, *"For all of you who were baptized into Christ have clothed yourselves with Christ. There is neither Jew nor Greek, there is neither slave nor free man, there is neither male nor female; for you are all one in Christ Jesus."* (Galatians 3:27 and 28)

The spurt in Church growth in South Korea and in the underground Church in China is being attributed to the releasing of women inside the Church.

It is also a proven fact that when women are given equal opportunities to education and employment, the economy grows.

This book is an attempt to unveil what has remained hidden for centuries in the name of family and societal honor- *the silent weeping of the Indian girls and women.*

Each story offers a sneak preview into the everyday lives of millions of girls and women and also shows the role Christians are playing and can play even further to bring about hope, healing, restoration and transformation.

As girls and women are stripped of their dignity, it is time for the Church to intervene and truly become the representative of Christ by asking, *"Woman, why are you crying?"* and bind their lacerated wounds.

I pray that this book will not only unveil the truth but also encourage us to prayerfully engage in reaching out for the upliftment of women, both spiritually and physically.

For I believe, *"History will have to record that the greatest tragedy of this period of social transition was not the strident clamor of the bad people, but the appalling silence of the good people."* -Martin Luther King Jr. in Stride towards Freedom.

God bless you.
Vinita Shaw
Founder/CEO
Disha Foundation

~ 1 ~

WOMB OR TOMB?

*"Hell begins the day God grants you the
vision to see all that you
could have done, should have done and
would have done but did not do."*
                    -Gian Carlo Menotti

India Prime Minister Dr. Manmohan Singh has termed the practice of female foeticide and infanticide in India a "national shame." According to Dr. Singh, "Improving the child-sex ratio is not merely a question of stricter compliance with existing laws but about changing how we view and value the girl child in our society."

My friend, Surinder, sounded frantic on the phone. Crying inconsolably, she babbled away. "I am pregnant but my husband has made it clear that if it is a female child, I have to abort!"

I was dumbfounded, "What are you saying? Are you in your right senses? When are you coming to Delhi? Did you tell your mother this?" I shot a volley of questions into the phone instrument.

Of course, I had to wait because my friend had hurriedly disconnected the phone, saying, "I will come and tell you every thing. Please do not tell anyone. My husband says this is a personal issue and he does not wish to discuss this or be judged by anybody."

It had only been four months since I happily bid goodbye to my good friend, Surinder. She had been getting on in age and the chances of her getting a good match were slimming by the day. At 30 years of age and still single, her parents were anxious.

"You are 30-years-old and still sitting on our head," was the remark her mother often threw at her, many times when I was around. I never did grasp the "sitting on head" concept, neither literally nor figuratively because Surinder was a big girl who could not possibly sit on anyone's head. Nor was she idle, as she had a good job in Chandigarh. Finally, they advertised in the newspaper and a family came to "see" Surinder.

The man had been a widower who was left behind with one young daughter. He was looking for a woman who would take care of his child since he kept a busy schedule.

Surinder hesitated, saying, "Not only is he older, but he has been married once. He will have memories of his first wife and will constantly compare her with me. It's not fair. I would like to marry someone who has not been married before. Moreover, I would like to marry someone I wish to marry, not someone I am forced to marry." But her mother had wept. "Please, Surinder. How long can we keep answering people's questions? We are embarrassed that you are still unmarried."

Surinder's mother's tears had melted her heart and she let her family have their way. Moreover, her husband-to-be was economically well off and would take good care of her, her mother had insisted, asking her to be practical.

Like most Indian girls, Surinder had given in to her mother's emotional blackmail.

And, now, barely four months after marriage, Surinder was in my house, sitting before me and crying. "I do not wish to abort my child. Whether it is male or female, it is my first child. I want to give birth to it. But my husband says that he already has a daughter from his first wife and in no way will he have another. I do not know what to do. He is a man of repute. He has threatened to send me back to my parents' house if I leak this matter out. He said he will quietly take me to the hospital one day on the pretext of a check-up where we can get an induced abortion if it is found to be a girl. He says he has a doctor friend who will tell us the sex of the child, although it is illegal."

She wept, hopelessly and helplessly.

"What are you going to do now?" I asked Surinder.

"I am not going to live with my husband if he forces me to abort my baby girl!" was her answer.

She was brave, but very alone, I mused as I looked at her determined jawline. However, the pressure from her mother was something she could not handle, "You must listen to your husband and mother-in-law. You must abort the child since we know you are going to birth a girl. You will not be respected if you have daughters."

I urged Surinder, "Did you seek your mother-in-law's help? After all, she is a woman. She will definitely stand for you."

"No way! My mother-in-law is the one who is pressuring my husband to abort if it is a girl."

"But where would she be if her parents had aborted her? Can she not think for herself?" I asked her.

Surinder cried on, helpless in the face of the stoic resistance. How she had looked forward to her first child!

And then it happened. While, her mother-in-law and husband were driving her to the clinic for an abortion, her husband turned on the nation's All India Radio's FM station called Rainbow to listen to some music. That is when they heard *"Khush Khabri,"* meaning good news. Peppered with music, containing information and entertainment, the program spoke on the after-effects of an abortion, giving facts that the doctor does not share with his patient. Side effects included cancer, excessive bleeding, giving birth to retarded children, depression, and suicidal tendencies. The program informed the listeners that the Lancet study estimates that more than 10 million female fetuses may have been aborted in India in the last two decades. The broadcast further informed that since modern technology has enabled sex-determining machines to reach even the remotest corners of India, that the slogan, "Pay Rs 500 now and save Rs 50,000 later in dowry" has led to millions of unnecessary abortions.

The program encouraged Indian parents to give birth to girl babies to prevent a personal, as well as a national catastrophe.

"That did it," she happily reported to me that day.

God saved me through that program. "My husband turned the car around halfway to the clinic, even as my mother-in-law sat silently in the car knowing the situation had gone totally out of her control."

Surinder had barely escaped the fate of millions of Indian women who have been forced to kill the girl baby in their wombs.

~ 2 ~

TRASHED

"What would men be without women?
Scarce, Sir, mighty scarce."
                    -Mark Twain

It was a dark, cold night in one of New Delhi's posh areas. People were rushing home to find respite from the cold and dry winter and the markets were beginning to wear a deserted look.

People had made such a hue and cry lately when the Chief Minister had ordered that markets be shut down by 7 p.m. They had protested, saying that they will have no time to shop. "There is no point in keeping the shops opened till late night, waiting for the office-goers to come and shop, because of the biting cold, there is nobody around," Samuel muttered under his breath, thrusting his hands deeper into his pockets for warmth, almost to the point of tearing them.

Samuel's shop was in the corner, and as he saw the crowds melting away, he wryly looked at his watch and then at the sky. It was only early December but due to the good rain Delhi had after a dry period of 10 years, the weather department said this winter was going to be severe. Samuel pulled his coat closer to his body and shoved his hands back into his pockets. Once he gets home to his wife and family, he will be fine.

His wife will make sure he is comfortable. She will have a hot water bath and hot food waiting for him. He had two fine boys who eagerly awaited his return every day. His wife kept a nice home for him and he was lucky to have her.

He'd wait an hour more, he decided. One could never tell. He might just get some shoppers his way. After all, he was running a general store with all types of items.

Having made up his mind, Samuel sat down and switched on the radio on his headphones and whistled along, listening to some film music. He had almost begun to doze off when he saw a couple of dogs behaving strangely. They were near a garbage bin and were making all kinds of noises, but they weren't barking. Curious, Samuel strolled towards the bin. They sniffed it and then began to roll it around. Samuel thought he heard the sound of a baby and turned around to see if some shoppers had finally come to his shop, but his shop was empty. Where did he hear a baby whimper?

He looked back at the dogs as they played football with the tightly rolled black packet. In spite of the darkness, Samuel saw movement from inside the packet. Initially, he thought some urchins had played a trick and wrapped a little puppy or a kitten to suffocate.

Kind as Samuel was, he could not bear to see a living being be suffocated to death. As he approached, the dogs barked at him menacingly. He picked up a stone to drive them away.

"I will release the little pet. I cannot see it being killed. Maybe, if it is a fine little animal, I will take it for my children as a pet," Samuel said to himself.

As Samuel began to unwrap the black plastic packet, not only did the being inside move, but also let out a little cry.

Samuel stopped mid-way. It was a frail human cry.

"No! No! It must be the purring of a baby kitten which must be missing its mother," Samuel said to himself as he quickly moved his fingers to open the packet.

There inside the large black plastic bag, he saw a sight he will not forget for as long as he lives. He saw a human baby, a newborn girl draped in a light cotton cloth.

"Oh, no, what is this? Who has committed such a grave sin? How can someone throw a newborn baby girl in the garbage? She is not dead. She is alive and she is not a pup or a kitten, but a human being!"

He quickly looked around and found himself all alone.

Pulsating silence followed. The dogs watched him from a distance as he carefully wrapped the baby again. "What should I do?" he asked himself. "This is a human baby who has been left to die in this severe cold if not eaten by the dogs."

It did not surprise him though, because he was very aware of the Indian society's intense love for the boy child. He remembered hearing on the *"Khush Khabri"* broadcast about newborn male babies being stolen from the hospitals because they fetched a high price with parents who had no sons. Also, what came to his mind was the throwing of female fetuses in the wells and fields of India. The broadcast had informed about the "girl deficit" which was more common among the educated families, especially in homes where the first-born child was a girl.

"No society can survive without women. This ghastly practice of trashing female babies is a violation of human rights and puts a question mark on our integrity as human beings," Samuel remembered the expert on the broadcast saying.

"And I wish so much for a daughter," he said to himself.

Either this girl was thrown away as trash because she was born out of wedlock and the mother feared being socially ostracized or the little girl was discarded because the family already had girls.

Samuel weighed his options. Since no one had noticed him with the packet, he could quickly wrap it back again and leave it where he found it. Or he could take the baby girl to the police station and hand her over.

It took only a moment for Samuel to make up his mind as the newborn cuddled closer to his bosom for warmth, as if she knew that this man would protect her from everything, including the cold.

Samuel would take this child as his daughter.

Lata is the name they gave her and she quickly became the joy of their home. Samuel, his wife and two sons are dark and short. Lata is very fair with beautiful brownish, black dancing eyes. Each time Samuel looks at her, he thanks God for this precious girl child whom he saved from the trash one cold, dark night.

"Lata is a gift from God for me and my family," Samuel proudly says beaming from ear to ear.

~ 3 ~

Unsafe Haven

*"The character of a country is known by
the way it treats its women."*
*-Jawaharlal Nehru,
first Prime Minister of India*

Sheena is the coordinator for a non-profit's project that helps women in need in Hyderabad, Andhra Pradesh. Tall, bold and confident, she counsels women rescued from trafficking to have courage and take control of their life's situations. Her counsel is effective because she practices what she preaches, i.e., to forget what is behind and move on to help others who are in similar conditions. This is what she told us.

"My parents separated when I was barely 4. I am told they were a handsome young couple, very much in love. My mother, barely 18, had been a runaway bride since her parents did not permit her to marry at such a young age. She had come with one suitcase to my grand parents' home, and marriage to my father followed.

After the birth of my younger brother, my father's job kept him very busy. He was away from home for long hours and my mother began to get lonely. During those long days and nights of waiting for my father, my mother became desperate. One day, she complained to my father's best friend about how lonely she gets at home, trapped with two little children. The friend understood her dilemma and offered to get rid of her loneliness by filling in for my father's long absence. He did a good job, because my mother abandoned my father and me, leaving me with my father and taking my younger brother away with her.

Nobody in the family wanted to take responsibility for me. The simple reason was that both of my parents were alive but each had lives of their own. However, off and on they managed to keep tabs on what was going on in my life, but without taking any responsibility.

This made it even worse. People would have taken me in if I had been an orphan, but being the child of living yet irresponsible parents was very tough on me. I missed them immensely. At every school function, while the other children expectantly waited for their parents. I waited too, but no one ever turned up. My father and mother had each re-married and had their own lives.

I was put in a Christian boarding school which permitted me to visit my uncle and his family only during holidays.

I looked forward to visiting since my cousin was my age and she shared her toys with me. We used to have fun. But one night, as I slept with my cousin, my uncle woke me up in the dead of the night.

Initially, I did not understand but then I did because at our boarding school, we had been taught the difference between a good touch and a bad touch. He was the elder brother of my father, very responsible, had a wife and children, and had the respect of people in the community.

Deep in the night, when the family slept, he would creep in my bed and try to fondle me. During the daytime, my aunt and cousin would leave and I would be left alone with him. On some pretext or the other, he would go to the office late. That is when I was most in danger.

How I hated the sight of him. He was a tall, strong and heavy-set man. He warned me that if I ever told anyone, he would kill me.

Day after day and night after night, I endured this torture.

Who would believe me? My parents do not have the time for me. Where do I go for help? I am all of 12-years-old," I thought to myself.

Days passed and, one day, I could not take it any longer. I called up my school principal and told her about the abuse. She raised a hue and cry. She informed some friends of the danger I was in. When confronted by family friends, my aunt shielded my uncle, saying that it is my irresponsible mother who was attempting to character assassinate her husband."

"How can she be so blind?" I wondered. Or did she

know and yet turned a blind eye? Was she protecting her family honor in spite of what she knew to be true?

I left their home and found refuge with a kind Christian family who welcomed me into their home during my school holidays. They saw me through college and helped me to become self-reliant.

To this day, my uncle's family believes that my mother had instigated me to character assassinate my uncle, hence, they will have nothing to do with me.

There are thousands of girls like me who suffer within their family and are damaged for life. Nobody believes them. Many commit suicide. Just as I was given refuge, I wish to offer refuge to as many as I can."

~ 4 ~

"Nakusha" – Unwanted

*"No one can make you feel
inferior without your consent."*
-Eleanor Roosevelt

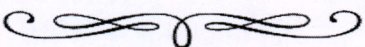

"You have a daughter and she is beautiful!" announced the hospital nurse, beaming with joy, as she handed over the newborn, all fresh and pink, to the mother. "Another failure," the mother thought to herself with deep disappointment as she turned her eyes away from the infant.

The nurse, a Christian, assuaged the mother, "Thank God for a healthy and normal child. She is God's gift to you. God has made boys and girls in His own image. Both are needed for carrying on of the human race. Both are very important. There are millions who do not have a child. Just look at her." But the mother stubbornly refused to even look at the child.

The grandfather, waiting in the hall outside the maternity ward, looked anxiously at his solemn-looking wife as she came out of the delivery room with a long drawn face, "What happened?"

"The same thing that happens every time. It is another girl – her third girl!" came the pat response in an angry tone. Everyone fell silent.

The baby girl was named Nakusha, which means "unwanted." There were other girls in the village with the same name.

Nakusha grew up in a small city in Maharashtra with her two older sisters, always eating their leftovers, wearing their worn-out clothes, and using their old books. She loved to play, and each time she had to be called back home, "Nakusha, come home!" rang out loud and clear for one and all that this girl was never wanted, yet she existed.

She was unwanted from the moment of her birth. She was reminded day-in and day-out by her parents, her family and her friends that she had not been wanted.

"I wish I had drowned you in the tub I had bathed you in. I am so ashamed to tell people that I have three daughters. They laugh behind my back. I wish you had died at birth," is the volley of words she received from her mother. These words came from her natural mother, not a stepmother.

Nakusha would yell back, "Why did you give me birth? Did I ask you to bring me into this world?" and her mother would be speechless and even more angry.

How Nakusha hated herself. She often cried herself to

sleep at night. "Nobody loves me. I wish I could go and throw myself in front of the trucks. Why is it my fault? What have I done to deserve such a fate? It is so insulting to be reminded day-in and day-out that I was never wanted. I wish I were dead!"

At the same time, Nakusha felt bad for her parents. Both had small jobs and they worked very hard to make ends meet. To add to their miserable existence was the burden of getting three girls married off, but no one would marry them unless they had a dowry to give. The future was bleak and the father would often vent his anger on the mother for giving birth to three daughters and then drink himself to sleep.

Then one day, he disappeared.

"Coward," Nakusha's mother called him as they wailed when he did not return home for days.

Nobody knew where he had gone. Did he commit suicide or get killed? Nobody knew. Even the local police did not bother to register a complaint.

Nakusha was blamed further for bringing bad luck to the family. Years passed, life had been unkind to her mother. After the father's disappearance, the burden of raising three young girls had taken a heavy toll on the mother's health. She had become frail and depressed. The torrent of angry words no longer rang in their little home; only a deep oppressive silence reigned.

This depression took its toll and the eldest daughter packed her bags one night to join a circus group that had come into the village. A short time later, the second daughter also packed her bags and disappeared. Some villagers said they had seen her board a bus for the big city.

The only one left behind was Nakusha.

"You also go and make a life for yourself. Do not waste your time on me. I will die soon," her mother whispered to Nakusha.

"No, Ma, I will not leave you. I will look after you," Nakusha lovingly said as she gently massaged her mother's legs and patiently fed her lentil soup day after day.

"I will not let you die, Ma. I love you, Ma. You will get well soon."

Silent and helpless, Nakusha's mother looked at her third daughter whom she had cursed since her birth. She knew she was alive only because Nakusha had taken responsibility for her and the home. And she remembers the words of the Christian nurse who had brought the third new born daughter to her saying,"She is God's gift to you ."

Today, she thanks God for Nakusha.

~ 5 ~

VANISHED

"Parents can only give good advice or put them on the right paths, but the final forming of a person's character lies in their own hands."
-Anne Frank

Neena was a pampered child, all of her 14 years. Her family was well-to-do with her father's business of exporting precious and semi-precious stones. Peels of laughter and cheer often rang in the home as family and friends were frequent visitors.

With a light complexion, large dancing black eyes that said as much as her little mouth did, a dimple on both cheeks, straight shoulder length hair, and a slender, well-shaped 5-foot-6-inch body, Neena was a treat for the eyes of one and all, and Neena was very conscious about it. From childhood, she had heard people exclaim, "Oh, what a lovely child," and that had given her airs.

She loved practicing to walk as if she were on the ramp, and it was a treat for one and all in the small city of Jaipur to watch her. She was the only girl child of her parents. With an older brother, the whole family doted on her.

"She will soon get married and move away," her parents would remark. Already, good families of their town with even better financial statures were eyeing Neena. "The earlier we marry her off, the easier she will adjust to the new home," her parents would often say within her hearing. Neena would vehemently oppose the thought. "OK, OK, we will not rush you into marriage," they would say in front of her, but they seriously thought about her marriage even as Neena considered her bright future. She had dreams of her own.

Those were dreams she knew were of no consequence to her parents. She could not think of a life decorated like a bride every day of her life. A life of walking with her head covered, wearing bracelets on her henna-covered arms, and rings and musical trinkets on her feet as she served food while producing a brood of children and living like her mother and grandmother did, a mere showpiece. No way, she said to herself.

Neena aspired to be a movie star and go to Bollywood.

Even during her growing-up years, Neena liked to admire herself in the mirror. She would put the table fan on full speed, making her lovely brown hair fly around her beautiful face, and would pose and smile, just as the actresses did in the Hindi movies.

And then one day, Neena got her dream break. A

Bollywood film unit had come to Jaipur to audition fresh faces for their new blockbuster movie. Neena was beside herself. However, she knew that her parents would not even allow her to go for an audition. When she was a child, they had scolded her many times for having such silly aspirations and this upset her.

Her brother could dream and have the full support of their parents, but not her. She was a girl. "Do not compare yourself to him," they would chide, offering no further explanations.

An older girl from her neighborhood planned an evening getaway to the hotel to secretly audition. Neena asked permission to go with her "to watch the film shooting" and because her parents knew the family well, they approved. Off the girls went, dressed in their latest clothes, to the hotel "to watch the film shooting."

Sleep eluded her from the time she visited the Bollywood set and auditioned. The lights, the sound, the director, the actors, and camera boys, the make-up artists and the ambience had left her head over heels in love. Furthermore, Neena had been given the business card of the casting director and Neena could not believe her luck. She knew her good looks would definitely help her find her way to the big screen.

So, not able to wait any longer, Neena plotted her escape by contacting the casting director. She set-up a day to meet with him for more auditions. Not a soul would know what was going on in her mind. Her parents and her friends, nobody knew of what she was plotting. She packed her bag, helped herself to some cash from her mother's purse, and boarded the train to Mumbai. Wearing sunglasses, high heels and trendy clothes, she hid her 14 years of age to a great extent. She met many young boys and girls on their way to Mumbai – the city that sells dreams. The casting crew director met her at the station. She could not believe her good luck. He said he had just left the auditions to come and pick her up from the train. She was taken to a posh hotel where he asked her to get ready for her audition for a film.

"Don't be nervous. These are all big-time producers. Just practice a few seductive poses and memorize these dialogues. They will love you," the director said.

Neena was excited. It was like a thousand butterflies had been let lose in her stomach. She rehearsed the dialogues and then she was taken to a large beautiful house where she acted as told. She did find it a little odd that all the men in the room whom she thought were producers were introduced to her as doctors, lawyers, politicians, and professors. There were no cameras around. No studio lights. There was just a large room where a heavily adorned woman sat on a couch chewing tobacco and playing with her flowered hair. Confused, she still did not grasp what was happening when, one by one, each man lifted his hand and said, "50,000, 100,000." Finally, the deal was settled with Rs 200,000.

"This is your first signing amount for the movie," said the casting director.

Confused, alone and not knowing what to believe and what not to believe, Neena was led to an underground room by the man who had "signed" her. There, her nightmare began.

Neena was to learn later that she had been auctioned and the highest bidder took her into a nightmare from where she never did wake up. She was kept drugged and forced to service customers. Finally, she was taken to a Middle East country to be a sex slave.

To this day, her parents have not discovered what happened to her. She just vanished into thin air, leaving behind no trace.

~ 6 ~

NIPPED IN THE BUD

"If by strength is meant brute strength, then, indeed, woman is less brute than man."
                                        -Mahatma Gandhi

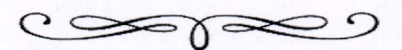

"Kallo, come home," yelled her mother. It was a hot day and Kallo had been playing in the sun with the other children from the neighborhood.

After calling her many times, the mother had to wrist-cuff Kallo to bring her back home, scolding her, "You want to get bronzed. Aren't you dark enough already?"

"But I want to play," the child said, resisting and stomping her feet in anger. Her mother chided her, "No, you silly girl. You should grow up now. You will soon be married."

"Kallo" (meaning Blackie in Hindi), was going to be 10 and her parents were frantically looking for a suitable match for her. They were worried because, at her age, most girls were married. She had trouble finding a match because she had a dark complexion.

Kallo was a sad child because her mother and everybody else in her family thought of her as ugly. "We are looking for a fair girl for our boy," families would insist.

And then, one day, finally, they found a husband for her, a 40-year-old man who already had three children. He wanted a wife who would keep his house, clean, prepare food, and also help him in the field.

The ten year old was very happy on her wedding day because her mother and father were happy. Kallo fell asleep during the ceremony because she was so tired with all the rituals and ceremonies that had preceded the wedding. Her mother mentally prepared her. "Kallo, after marriage, your husband's home is your home. You should never leave it and come back to us. You can only leave your husband's house when you die. Only your dead body can leave his house. Understand very clearly."

Little wonder that at her departure, her parents cried as if she were dead. They would not be seeing her anytime soon. Maybe, they would see her once in a while when her husband would bring her or when they would visit. Naturally, they would not even drink the water from her home, let alone eat there. They believed that it was a sin to eat and drink in the daughter's home.

Kallo wept when she saw her husband. He was old enough to be her father. Her wedding night and all the nights thereafter were a nightmare. Every morning, she was forced to take the cows out, feed them, cook, and do the household chores. Kallo's married life had begun. It was a living hell. Everybody in the family, which included her elder brother-in-law and father-in-law, had the right to hit her, kick her, rape her, and abuse her.

Time passed and Kallo continued to suffer. She had no way out. Her parents had tutored her, saying that only her dead body would leave the husband's house. How she wanted to run away. How she wanted to end her life. Tiny as she was, there was no escape for her. She hated herself and her life. She wished she could kill them all. As she grew, the hatred inside her grew, too. Then, as if her desires came true, dacoits raided the village, killing many men, one of them being her husband. What a relief, but that was short-lived, too. They carried the girls away and she was among them. As months became years, Kallo grew used to the rough living with the dacoits. One day, Kallo asked the head dacoit to teach her how to shoot. He hesitated, but taught her anyway. He was surprised how good she was at it. "Was it her natural talent for shooting or the hatred that made her aim so clear?" he thought to himself and smiled.

"Come with us next time we go on a raid."

Kallo was overjoyed.

Wielding the gun gave her immense pleasure. It was now that she had power. Time was on her side and she was trigger happy.

Kallo grew used to the rough ways of living with the dacoits until one day, in an encounter with police; she was killed with the rest of them.

Kallo was barely 25.

~ 7 ~

PRECIOUS GIRLS

*"Dare to reach out your hand into the darkness,
to pull another hand into the light."*
                            -Norman B. Rice

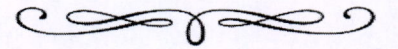

It was a bright and warm day in a little village of Rajasthan, the desert state of India. As the sun beat mercilessly, not a soul was visible outside on the narrow mud lanes. One and all were taking a siesta. Apart from a few trucks that traveled on the national highways, leaving behind a cloud of dust, there was no movement. Rupa lay under a fan in her small house, as others slept off the afternoon heat.

Rupa was seven months pregnant. This was her first child and her husband was very excited, as was everyone else in her joint family. Everyone indulged Rupa, saying, "Eat this special dish I have prepared. Drink milk, as it will be good for the baby, keep your legs up and take rest," and so on and so forth.

Everybody was praying for a daughter. Rupa and her family lived in Rajasthan, the desert land of India and belonged to the Bedia tribe. They believed that the women in their families were born to be sex workers. Light brown skin, hazel eyes, long hair and colorful clothing marked them out. The red, green, orange and yellow colors made the brown arid landscape look better when the beautiful women of the Bedia tribe began their dance.

From childhood, the girls here are trained to be prostitutes, sometimes as early as 8-years-old. They are taught to dress up, walk, and dance so as to entice men so they could do a good business for the family.

Rupa was being pampered and a lot of expectations were placed on her. Rupa herself was a sex worker but was taking a holiday to rest and give birth to a beautiful girl child who would then continue the family business. Their little hamlet was next to the national highway and it was normal for the women of the village to service truck drivers while the husbands sat around puffing away at their *hookah* (a rural-style, long-stemmed cigarette) and children played outside the house.

Although the government was announcing schemes to educate the girl children of the village, Rupa was not interested. Even a Christian non-profit organization had opened a project in their area in which they were giving awareness on AIDS, but she was determined to train her daughter in the ways of being a prostitute. Thanks to scientific inventions, there were now injections available in the village which would ripen the little girl into a fully mature woman. That would mean they would have a steady income for years to come. Rupa was already counting the eggs even before they were hatched. With a smile playing on her lips and a gentle pat on her abdomen, Rupa slithered deeper into her cot to rest herself and propped her legs up on the colorful cushions that lay below her feet.

A neighbor who had moved to Mumbai had introduced them to the special injection with a drug called Oxytocin which he said was available easily at the chemists' shops in the villages and near-by towns as well.

"Usually, it is given to cattle since they produce more milk when given. But if we give it to our little girls, they will mature faster. So, you can calculate how much income they will get for you without your having to wait until they actually mature."

All the villagers were delighted with this new gained-knowledge. Soon, they would begin to test on their daughters. He further informed them, in his typical pompous way of a man who had been to the big city as the villagers gaped at him with their eyes and mouth wide-opened: "I found out about this injection from people in Mumbai and Pune. I also saw the girls who developed into voluptuous full-bodied women. We can begin to give them Oxytocin from age 8 onwards."

Somebody had even told Rupa that a girl as young as six-months-old can also fetch a good price. "Those people will raise her as their own daughter," but Rupa immediately rejected the idea. She'd like to keep the baby to herself. After all, this was the first time Rupa was going to be a mother and she wanted to enjoy her first child. How she yearned for a daughter, whom she would bathe with scented perfume water and milk, put kohl in her eyes, oil and flower her hair, pierce her ears and nose, and give her small trinkets to wear when she would run around the house. She smiled and patted her abdomen and drifted into a deep, blissful sleep.

~ 8 ~

GODDESS OF TRASH

*"Past experience should be a guiding
post, not a hitching post."*
                    -D.W. Williams

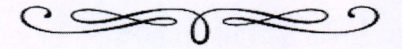

While doing a series of weekly classes on value education and character building at a Christian girls' hostel, we had been talking for three weeks in a row about the superstitious beliefs in India. The excited girls, about 20 of them, all wanted to speak at the same time, about the following beliefs which they had been tutored with from their homes.

A black cat crossing your path means bad luck.
If you sneeze before going out, it is unlucky.
If you eat from the cooking vessel,
    it will rain on your wedding day.
If you criss-cross the scissors, there is fight in the home.

If you keep one shoe on top of another,
   there will be a fight.
If you itch on your left palm you will get money.
If you itch on your right palm, your money will go.
And so on, and so forth.

As I took the girls on a journey to assess for themselves what they thought was true or false, depending on the education they were receiving, they laughed and giggled as they came to a self-realization about what they had been tutored by their families to believe.

Watching them arrive at the end of that journey was gratifying as they laughed and clapped, light shining in their eyes, finally understanding the lies that they had believed all along.

When we reached the final session on the series and I was about to wind up, Suzzanna stood up. A big-bodied girl from Ranchi, she is a student of class IX. With round cheeks and a shy smile, she had been listening and smiling for a long time before she said, "We have been told that if you clean your house after dark, the goddess will go away. Is it true?"

Not wanting to spoon feed them, I asked them to put their thinking caps on.

I asked her if trash is good or bad. She said it was bad.

"Well, why is it bad?" I asked.

"Because it stinks and can cause sickness"

"Well, then whether it is day or night, you just get rid of it. What have you learned at school about cleanliness?"

"Cleanliness is next to godliness."

"Well, then, you say the goddess likes to live in trash."

"So, we have to keep our surroundings clean and not believe that the goddess wants to live in the trash."

Then she smiled, lowered her eyes, looked at me and smiled. It was like a light had fallen on her mind.

"Mother, we are three sisters and now we have a little brother. My parents love our brother more than us. Why is this so ?" asked Sagrika, a twelve year old from the corner of the room

"God has created man and woman in His own image and He loves both. So, do not believe if you are told that you are a burden and a liability or made to feel that way. You are not. You are precious."

And they all smiled.

The other day I visited them after a gap of few weeks' time and they came running to me. One of the bolder ones, Muskan, asked me, "Mother, first answer my question. Why have you not been coming for the past few weeks?"

I smiled. Were these the same girls I had begun teaching two years back; shy, reserved and steeped in dark thinking. No, not any more. Light was beginning to shine on them and darkness was departing.

~ 9 ~

LEGACY OF AIDS

"Birds sing after a storm, why shouldn't we?"
               -Rose Kennedy

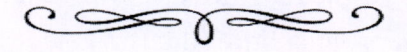

❦

"We are four sisters and one brother. My father died when I was barely 10 years. My mother is very sick and is on treatment," is a short introduction that Nisha gives of her family. Miserably thin, with weak hair, but with large eyes which show determination and courage, Nisha does not have the time to be frivolous like her younger siblings. Finishing her final year of college, she has plans to get an accountant's job and help her family. Regular listeners of the radio broadcasts of Disha Foundation were very much touched by the broadcast on AIDS and women because Nisha's mother got AIDS from her husband and, today, she is slowly sinking.

This is what Nisha's mother told us.

"Initially, I was very bitter. We had been married for so many years. I thought he loved me. I had no way of knowing that he was visiting other women as well. We made a small house for ourselves, had children and then one day, he fell sick. On doing the routine blood tests, we discovered that he was on the last stage of AIDS. It was so shameful. We did not know how to handle it. We kept the news to ourselves, but couldn't do it very long. And then one day, accidentally, we heard a radio program on AIDS. They promised to keep our identity hidden and connected us to a local government hospital from where we got medicines, but we had come to know about the sickness very late. My husband died within a few months of the diagnosis, leaving me behind with four young daughters and a little son.

"My initial reaction was to commit suicide. Little did I know that there was more to come.

"I fell sick and thinking that my husband's demise had caused my sickness, I was shell-shocked when I came to know that I, too, had AIDS. I could not believe it. I had never been with any other man. I had known only my husband and it is then that it dawned upon me. It was so unfair, so very unfair. I wanted to die but looking at the faces of my young children, I had to muster up all my courage and carry on.

"We were called social lepers. Most of our family and friends totally disconnected from us. Even those who came would give a little money and disappear. They were so afraid that they would contract the deadly disease, too.

"My family had a bleak future. My daughters were

growing up. I had nowhere to turn. It was then that a Christian family came forward to help us. They not only visited us but also helped us to re-build our broken lives."

"Today, three of the girls are economically independent while two younger children are still in school. We have joined a local church where we are not despised but welcomed.

"Every day, there are reports about economically weak children and girls going missing and sold into sexual slavery. I worry for my children about what will happen to them after I die. The eldest daughter is only 24. I pray that God would grant me life until they are all grown up so I can rest in peace."

~ 10 ~

UNWED MOTHER

"If a child is not safe in her own mother's womb, where on earth can she be safe?"
                                              -Mother Teresa

It was 9 p.m in the city of Delhi, the capital city of the region of Delhi. Anita was getting ready for work. She would find it very odd initially because when every one in the family was coming home from work, she was just leaving for work. Anita worked nights at the call center.

Having been abandoned by her father, she and her mother shared a small house with her maternal grandmother and the family of an aunt. With one small toilet and two tiny rooms, they spent most of the time out of the home, especially with the hot temper and sharp tongue of her octogenarian grandmother. Living in that house and growing up there, seeing her mother weep and her grandmother tongue-lash her for marrying a man who abandoned her soon after she became pregnant, Anita had often wished to run away.

And she did run away, but only in her dreams. She would daydream and find comfort in them, even if it was for a little while. She dreamt that one day she would have a home of her own, with a husband who would always love her and never ever abandon her. Although her mother was bitter toward all men, Anita believed that there was a good man somewhere out there who would be her prince on a white horse.

After all, not all men were like her father. No, there were also responsible men who looked after their families, held on to jobs and took their children to school and got them married. How she wished some such man would love her and give her all that she had not received thus far – the protection and security of a man – so much a necessity in Indian society.

"Even if there is no man in the house but his shoes are sitting in the house, it is enough for people to know that there is a man here and to behave themselves," she had heard her neighbor say at the funeral of a man who had left behind only a wife and daughter.

Anita very much missed her father, whom she had never seen. She guessed he was a fair man because her mother was a very dark woman yet Anita had a light brown complexion. She had not even been told his name nor shown a picture of the man who fathered her.

"To love and raise the child of a man who had abandoned you, and a child who looked like him, you are a stupid woman. You should throw her in the orphanage," Anita had often heard her grandmother and aunt advise her mother. But her mother had her way. She worked very hard to raise Anita, wishing to give Anita a happy life, something she did not have.

Living in the city of Delhi with a growing population of about 16 million, jobs for graduates were not easy to come by. After many efforts, Anita joined a call center which kept her at work in the night and allowed her hardly any sleep at home during the daytime.

It was at the call center that she met Rahul, a nice young man, a couple of years older than her. They were attracted to each other and because of the number of hours they spent at work; they soon began to hang out together. They would visit the local parks and spend hours soaking in the Delhi's winter sun. They shared their dreams and plans for their future.

Rahul's father, too, had abandoned his mother, she soon learned, and a deep bond developed between them. They shared the hatred for their fathers and felt responsible for their mothers who had, with great difficulty, brought them up.

Anita was ecstatic. Finally, she had met the man of her dreams!

With the passage of time, Rahul and Anita became intimate. And Anita got pregnant.

"Are you out of your mind? What do I do if you are pregnant? You should have taken precautions. Now, go to the doctor and abort the child," Rahul told her.

Anita was shocked. She looked at Rahul, open-mouthed.

"But I thought you loved me," she said, sobbing,

frightening Rahul further.

"Come on. What has this got to do with love? You and I both are not ready for marriage. We have family responsibilities and a call center job is just a temporary job for me. You know I am studying and would like to get a better job before I settle down."

Anita dare not tell her mother. She knew her mother would die. She knew her mother had expected her to be more sensible, knowing how her father had abandoned them. But Anita, being young and hopeful, had not anticipated that she, too, would be in her mother's shoes one day.

Anita had to make a decision. Even if she loved Rahul and wanted to keep the baby, it was totally out of question. The social stigma related to an unwed woman being pregnant was something her family would never come to terms with. Even more so because the history of an abandoned pregnant woman was still fresh in the mind of the family, as well as the neighborhood where they lived. Having studied in a Christian school, she was keenly aware that abortion is a sin in the sight of God. She had grown up learning about sanctity of life and was aware of the mental and physical after effects of abortion.

Yet, it was unfathomable, incomprehensible, and totally inconceivable to the Indian mind that a single unwed mother would give birth to a child.

Anita found her way to an abortion clinic, thousands of which thrive in the big cities of Delhi and terminated her pregnancy. She feigned sickness and slept for two days and then went back to work. Nobody needs to know, she thought to herself.

Today, Anita continues to trudge along with her life, knowing that being an Indian girl whose father abandoned her makes her vulnerable. She often contemplates suicide but lives on for her mother.

~ 11 ~

OF SATAN AND GIRLS

*"We must straighten our backs and work
for our freedom. A man can't ride
you unless your back is bent."*
                    -Martin Luther King Jr.

"We have been taught in our religion that as soon as a young girl leaves the house, Satan accompanies her," she said to me.

I wanted to burst out laughing in her face but looking at her serious face, I realized this was no joke and I restrained. I had never heard of a more outrageous thinking than this, I thought as I bit my lip in an attempt to arrest my smile. "What about all that Satan does inside the house," I wanted to ask, knowing all about the family's immoral life style.

I looked across at my colleague and we exchanged smiles.

We were visiting Shana's house, her mother, Mumtaz, was conversing with us as we had come to inaugurate a small tailoring business for them that would take them toward their journey towards self-reliance.

We were sitting on the fifth floor of a building which stood precariously. All illegal and earthquake prone, hidden behind the malls and freeways where traffic buzzes past, in a narrow lane, which is barely accessible, except for walking of two people at a time, there are houses built like match boxes. It is hard to believe but this was the capital city of Delhi, pretty much hidden.

Abandoned by her husband when Shana and her brother were mere toddlers, Mumtaz, is a bitter woman today. She had married for love, defying her conservative parents and eloped with her lover only to return after a few years when he deserted her, as well as their two children. Shana was sent off to a Christian boarding school in the city where she grew up. Thin, wiry, with weak hair, and large brown eyes, Shana preferred to stay to herself more often than not. Once in a while, she was taken to her mother, who now lived with her sister's husband and children as man and wife would. Since Mumtaz did not have any of education or job skills, when her brother-in-law offered a place to live, she accepted.

Shana never liked to go back there because there were eight people living with one small toilet and very little privacy. Having finished her schooling with a lack of finances did not make Shana very hopeful about her future. One of her friends had already left for the modeling world, which Shana found out later was flesh trade. The others had been married off to older men.

When Shana had no hope in life, the warden of the Christian hostel introduced her to Disha Foundation, which put her through college and gave her a high-level professional course in fashion design. Also, Disha gave Shana her first tailoring job as a teacher to the hostel girls. After more than 15 months, Shana was provided with high commercial machines so that, together with her mother, Shana could start a small business of her own.

Mumtaz is adamant to get Shana married and get rid of her burden; but Shana would like to become financially independent before she marries a man she would choose for herself.

Shana does not believe in talking much but she has a mind of her own, which is pretty much made up. She has seen and heard enough about the crimes against girls like her and, with God's help, wishes to be self-reliant.

~ 12 ~

KIDNEY FOR SALE

"A successful woman is someone who takes all the bricks others have thrown at her and makes a firm foundation."
                              -Anonymous

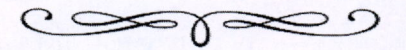

Antra was exhausted. Her blind mother had finally fallen asleep and so had her drunkard brother. It had been an evening of loud shouting, crying and cursing. She could hear her sister-in-law sobbing softly in the other room, as tonight she had been the victim of her husband's wrath. The atmosphere was choking Antra. There was so much toxicity around her, even in the air. She just had to get out of the house and out she ran into the December cold air of New Delhi. Little did she know at that time, that Nirbhaya, a 23-year-old girl, was being brutally raped on the streets of the same city by four men. It could have been Antra's fate, too, as

Delhi had been labeled as the rape capital of India, but Antra was oblivious.

This had become a daily routine for the 25-year-old girl. But things had not always been like this, she had once been a happy young girl living in Delhi with her family. True, Antra had not been good at studies, she was a school dropout, but her family had a small house that her father had built. Her older sister was married and living in another Indian city with her family. Some years back, her mother had to be operated upon and that is when her optic nerve was accidentally cut by the doctor. Being semi-illiterate, they did not know how to seek compensation or which door to knock on. Finally, the family reconciled to the fate that the mother will always be blind and will need to be cared for until her death. At least they were together and the family took turns looking after the mother.

Things took an ugly turn when, last year, Antra's father suddenly passed away, leaving Antra and her mother at the mercy of a drunkard brother who was also an abusive husband and father. He took no responsibility for the family, nor did he provide financial help as one would have expected from the son of the house. After all, Indians prayed for a son so that he would take care of them in their old age and attain salvation for them after death.

But here, Antra's brother was no blessing, rather a curse for the mother, sister and wife. He would often get into drunken brawls and not return home many nights. He would get violent if any of the women would dare ask him for money or remind him of his responsibilities. He was angry that his scheme to sell off the house was met with stoic resistance by Antra.

In such a condition, it fell upon the shoulders of young Antra to provide for her family. She had a small sewing machine at home and had trained as a tailor when her father was alive. She had the certificates which could help her get a job or she could also work as a shop assistant. After all, Delhi is a very big city and there are girls seeking an education or a job every day in this bustling city. True, there were risks involved because girls belonging to economically weak families were often raped and exploited.

But due to her mother's total child-like dependence of her, Antra had no way of going out to even attempt to look for a job. Sometimes, with the anger and emotions welling up inside her, and her hungry stomach growling, she would run out of the house. How she wished to end her life. How she wished someone would kill her.

Days turned into months until one night, after the family had fallen asleep on half a stomach, Antra lay wide awake playing with her small mobile phone. She put it on FM-All India Radio Rainbow on which was playing a program called *"Khush Khabri,"* meaning good news. Wondering what good news there was, she listened to the program discussing the situation of women in India. The program encouraged girls and women to have a positive approach towards life. Hoping for help, she wrote a little text message asking the radio program to advertise for her. Antra wanted to sell one of her kidneys for money and she asked Disha Foundation to advertise this on their broadcasts.

A week later, a representative of Disha Foundation visited with Antra. She was a young, small, dark-looking girl with such a weak economic background that she would easily be a target for the traffickers in Delhi. And sure enough, Antra confided, "There were men who had already offered one-night stands in exchange for helping her."

Thanks to her new friends of Disha Foundation, Antra was provided with a big sewing machine, on her request, so that she could grow her sewing business. Along with connections to people that place orders for clothing, Antra also receives financial assistance every month and will continue to do so until she is self-reliant.

Antra is smiling today and wrote a long text to Disha Foundation saying, "Thank you very, very, very, very, very, very, very, very, much." Antra has recently been appointed as the tailoring teacher for a hostel that Disha Foundation supports.

~ 13 ~

MUCH ADO ABOUT "I DO"

*"Life shrinks and expands in
proportion to one's courage."*
            -Anais Nin

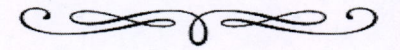

The atmosphere in the house was stifling, partly because of the June heat and partly because of Seema's mother. She was again nagging.

Seema's parents were anxious. They had all the reasons to be. Their daughter was going to be 26 and was still not married. So what, if they lived in a big Indian city and their daughter was well educated and had a good job? They were embarrassed each time somebody asked them, "Is your daughter still not married?"

"What is the big deal?" Seema would get angry with her parents. "Can't I live my own life? Can't I decide when and whom to marry?"

"Please, Seema," her mother would begin to cry. "How long can you sit at home? People keep asking us. It is our responsibility to marry you off. We live in a society and have to follow the societal norms. Once we marry you off, we will go and bathe in the holy river of Ganges."

"What did the river Ganges have to do with her getting married or not getting married?" Seema angrily retorted.

"Neither am I sitting at home nor a burden on you. I have a good job. I do not want to rush into a marriage and regret it later. I would like to marry someone I love and not be pushed into marrying a total stranger."

"That is unthinkable," her mother would say to her. "If your father hears, he will kill you."

And then both the women would cry their heart out before getting ready for another party to come and "see Seema."

"Am I a cow or a piece of furniture? Why do they want to see me, reject me and then go away? I hate it so much. I feel like an object. I feel like running away from the house."

Her pleas fell on deaf ears. "That is how I married your father. I first saw his face on our wedding night and it is alright. That is the way marriages are arranged in our society," her mother consoled her.

Once again, Seema was readied for inspection. She was dressed in a lovely Indian sari and ushered into the room with a tray carrying tea. The pink sari set off her dark complexion, making it look lighter. Once she served everyone tea, she looked up to see five pair of eyes assessing her from head to toe.

After a thorough examination and a lot of questions, to which Seema responded in monosyllables of "yes" and "no," the prospective mother-in-law took Seema's chin into her hands and said, "She is nice, but she is dark. How much dowry will you give?"

Seema seethed inside. She was a working girl, having been through university. Why were they asking for dowry?

Wouldn't she be the hen that lays a golden egg every month? How she loathed this system of dowry which made Indian parents treat daughters like an economic burden.

"Our son has an MBA. We have spent a lot of money on his education. Naturally, we want to be reimbursed," asserted the mother-in-law as if reading Seema's thoughts.

Seema looked at her parents as they looked helplessly at her prospective in-laws with folded hands and an apologetic look on their faces. Her dark complexion was a bane for her. How many times she had been rejected because the demand for dowry was very high.

"We want a good car and 10 lakh rupees. If you agree, we will fix the marriage date right now."

After they left, her mother comforted her. "Don't worry. We have heard your husband is a good man and the dowry will bring you respect in your new home."

"But giving and taking dowry is illegal," wailed Seema and I do not even know him or about him. "Please, do a background check on him first. Why are you in such a hurry to send me away?

"Please, Seema. Just cooperate with us. We have found out everything about him. He lives in another city.

"He has a good job and he will take you with him. He will look after you well. You can find another job there if you like," added the father.

On the wedding night, Seema's husband told her, "I have a relationship with another woman. I live with her. I love her and I have married you because of family reasons. We all will live together. You are my wife and will bear my children but you must never leak out this information to your family or mine."

Seema was kept locked in a room by her husband and his mistress. She had no access to a phone and was unable to contact her parents. Days turned into weeks and weeks into months, and finally when she did get an opportunity to call her mother and pour out her complaint to her, the mother's response was, "I am so sorry to hear this. It must be your fault that you are not able to win the favor of your husband. You are his legally wedded wife. One day, he will belong to you totally. Be patient."

The same night, Seema committed suicide.

~ 14 ~

HAPPY HOLIDAYS

"The best thing is that none of us need wait a single moment to help improve this world to be a better place."
　　　　　　　　　　　　　　-Anne Frank

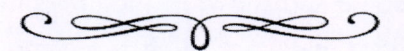

The following is a text we received for our radio program when we created awareness about the growing problem of Holiday brides in our country.

"I am from Punjab. I am one of the holiday brides. Why did you not air this program earlier? I would have saved myself from being duped. Now I suffer as my husband has disappeared, leaving me with a small child in a society that frowns at me for being a married, yet abandoned woman."

This is Balwinder's story:

"I come from a small village in Punjab. There are not many girls here. Since the ultrasound machines came here, the slogan that is marketed is, "Spend Rs 5,000 to abort a female fetus to save Rs 50,000 in dowry later."

And many opt for getting their pregnancy terminated if they are found to be carrying a girl.

People are poor here, largely illiterate, mostly farmers and they live in small houses. One thing that is very big on their minds is going to England or any foreign country. They may have never visited a city in India, but they dream to migrate overseas. There are many villagers whose sons are taxi drivers in England, the U.S. and European countries. They come back once in a year. Some bring their families back here. Girls who used to walk around with bare feet in the village are now wearing high-heeled sandals and a lot of gold jewelry and speaking a language that is "foreign" to us. They even look like foreigners.

They come and show off pictures of a life in a foreign land where they make so much more money compared to their fellow villagers.

Like other villagers, my brother and I also wished to migrate. My brother is hell bent on doing so. He keeps making connections with the villagers settled overseas and has been doing so for more than a couple of years but nothing has happened. He is frustrated. He hates to work in the field under the relentless sun and then wait for the crops to grow. He has been to the big cities of India and, hence, has dreams in his eyes to go overseas.

"You cannot imagine how beautiful and easy life is in a foreign land. There are nice houses, big trains and planes, big cars. You work hard and get a lot of money. Here, we work so hard and just eke out a living for ourselves. There is no future here," he tells me as I look at him with my doe-like kohl-filled eyes. My mouth is open in amazement. I continue to listen as I push back my long brown hair, drying in the sun, while sitting on the cot outside our habitation peeling onions for our evening meal.

  A week later, I received a proposal. All of 18 years I am and yet everyone is eager to see me off. The man, a taxi driver in Canada, had seen my picture taken at the wedding of my close friend here in the village. We had danced the whole evening of the wedding, singing the famous Bollywood songs with me in the lead.

  The groom and his family had come from Canada. After the wedding, they returned to Canada and showed the pictures and the video from the wedding to their family and friends. That is where the man's proposal had come from. "Which pictures," I asked my beaming mother who proudly showed me the wedding album that the proposer had brought along.

  I gasped at the colored glossies. I did not know I looked so pretty in green, with my long hair draped in colorful ribbons and my face shining with excitement, my make-up, henna and jewelry adorning me. I had been so busy dancing that I did not even realize that pictures had been taken.

  Even before I could respond, my brother, came bounding up to me, "Wow, what luck my beautiful sister has brought to our family! Imagine when you go overseas; you can call me, too. Our lives will change! Not only will you benefit, but our whole family will come out of this vicious cycle of poverty. After you go to Canada, you can send for me. I will work hard and send a lot of money home. Our parents can build a new house. Father will no longer have to work. Mother will also wear jewelry and finally, we will be very, very happy."

I agreed.

I saw the bridegroom on the wedding day. He was resplendent in green, red and gold, and mounted on a white horse. He was escorted down the roadside by a procession of merry men in pink turbans, bearing staffs of golden bells and colorful pennants. On his lap sat a little boy, perhaps a nephew, as a symbol to wish that only boys be born to this couple.

I was dressed in dark pink with lots of gold jewelry, all of which had been sent to me by the groom.

Amidst a lot of dances and bursting fire crackers, the bridegroom was led to the stage where the chairs were fit for a king and a queen. I was escorted to the stage and a procession of well-wishers filed past, dropping folds of rupee notes into an oversized bronze urn.

I stole a quick look at him. He was tall, fair and had a winsome smile. He wore a turban and his gaite was confident.

My friends and relatives had traveled hundreds of kilometers to attend my wedding and there were about 500 people in total at the ceremony.

My family had taken a big debt from the village money lender. "It is only a matter of a few months and we will return the money back with interest," said my brother. "After all, a man settled overseas is marrying my sister. We need to do things as per his standard," he had rambled on.

Everyone was delirious with happiness. We had not seen such extravaganza but we were getting ready for a prosperous life ahead.

The next morning, the whole village, along with my family, came to bid me goodbye as I started my new life with my husband in a big city of Punjab. He had come on a three-month holiday, he had told my parents.

"In these three months, I will do the paperwork from the big city which has a Canadian office so that I can take my wife with me."

With tears and dream-filled eyes, with tears for the past and dreams for a wonderful, promising future, I rode out into the unknown in my husband's luxury car.

My husband was a wonderful and kind man. He did not deride me for my rural ways. Rather, very patiently, he helped me change my wardrobe and hair style, taught me words of English and Canadian ways so I could adjust to a new life with him.

I was very happy.

After three months, he took me back to my parent's home, saying, "I have submitted all the migration papers but it is taking some time with the government of Canada. Not a problem, I will go back to Canada and push them from there. I have friends in high places. Until then, I am leaving my treasure with you. Please look after her well." He pushed a big bundle of Canadian dollars into my father's hesitant hands in the presence of my brother, who was beaming with joy.

My illiterate, poverty-stricken father and now debt-ridden father folded his hands in sheer gratitude and, with tears of joy spilling from his eyes, he hugged my husband.

"And you," said my husband to my brother, "get packing your bags. As soon as your sister comes to Canada, then it is your turn."

And to me, he whispered, "I love you. I will call you every week. You better be home when I call." He had embraced me as I evaded him, blushing at this brazen public display of affection.

My brother grinned from ear to ear. "It's okay. You are now his wife and this is the Canadian way of showing affection. Better get used to it."

After my husband's departure, our wedding pictures were my only source of comfort. I would gaze at them for hours and when we had electricity, I would pester my brother to borrow a movie player from the village shop so I could watch the film that was made of our wedding. Our family would laugh, as they were such happy memories captured on the CD.

I waited for his phone call.

Weeks turned into months.

"He must be very busy. He'll call."

My family comforted me.

"Why don't we call?" suggested my brother one day. We placed a call to the number he had given to us.

"There is no response, it says, 'There is no such number'." My brother informed me.

"Why don't you write a letter? I will bring the address," said my father.

I wrote a long letter and then a letter every day.

It has been five years and I have stopped writing letters now.

Giving me company are my wedding pictures and a son who looks exactly like his father.

My father has taken me from pillar to post, seeking help from police and government agencies but to no avail.

All we hear is, "You people are so greedy to migrate that you do not even check out the details before marrying your daughter off."

"We are poor and illiterate. We believe in people. What do we do now?" my father helplessly asks. He hangs his head in shame, unable to meet my eyes that once held dreams but are now shattered for life."

~ 15 ~

TORCHED ALIVE

*"To call women the weaker sex is a libel;
it is man's injustice to women."*
-Mahatma Gandhi

Seeing the charred body wrapped in a blanket, no one would have imagined what a lovely girl Usha had been. Since I admired her as a child in the neighborhood, I would also remember her as a very beautiful girl.

Fair complexioned, she had large black eyes, which usually remained down as she silently served her grandfather, father, mother, and younger brothers and sisters. From morning till night, she would work like a slave. There were no dishwashers, washing machines or blenders when I was growing up. She was sent to school, though only after finishing all household chores. When she did get some time for herself, I found her scrubbing her lovely feet or playing with little children. Although 18, she enjoyed playing with children in the evenings until the time her mother's angry screaming would beckon her home. Her mother was always yelling at her. I wondered why. But there is not much that I understood as a 6-year-old. I loved to watch Usha because her house was one floor below our apartment and I could watch her come out and go into the house.

We all attended her wedding. We had to because we were neighbors, but the custom was that since we were the girl's side, we would just give the cash gift and leave. This was the Indian way, by not attending the party, we wouldn't add to the financial burden of an average, lower-middle class family of the bride.

We went to see Usha before her wedding. She was all dressed in red and looked splendid. A red and gold sari adorned her and a large red dot stuck on her forehead. She had kohl in her eyes and henna painted on her palms and legs. She had red nail paint on her toes and fingernails. She was a sight to behold.

Little did I know that I would be seeing her for the last time.

I am told that two days later, she was burnt to death for not bringing enough money with her as dowry. Apparently, the father had promised to give more money and a car to the bridegroom and his family. This was over and above the lavish expenses incurred during the marriage ceremony and feeding the 1,000-plus guests who had come with the bridegroom. When the father failed to deliver, the new bride, his daughter, had to pay the price.

I heard the bridegroom is now happily married and has another wife.

Obviously, the new wife brought a lot of dowry with her, fulfilling the demands of her in-laws and, therefore, is happy and respected in her new home.

~ 16 ~

DARED TO LOVE

*"There are causes worth dying for,
but none worth killing for."*
— Albert Camus

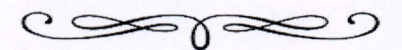

───※───

Veena's corpse hung from the tree in the center of the squalid little village in Haryana. When the police came to question her family, all they heard from the father and four brothers was, "This is our family matter and you have nothing to do with it." This was a village where even the police tread with much trepidation because centuries-old mindsets were far more important here than law and order.

This is what had happened to Veena:

It had been love at first sight for Veena.

He was a teacher in the local government school and came knocking at her door one lazy afternoon. Usually, Veena's lovely oval face remained hidden by a veil, especially when she went out of the home, but he had come at an odd hour. Crossing the courtyard hurriedly, she forgot to cover her face, not anticipating a male at this time of the afternoon. "Must be some woman from the neighborhood," she muttered to herself as she opened the door and looked directly into the face of a handsome young stranger.

Her heart did a little ballet.

Hurriedly, she tried to veil her face, but it was too late. The stranger looked straight at her face and smiled, which unnerved her more, and the more she hurried, the more difficulty she had securing the veil. The breeze played tricks with her too and her long hair frolicked around her forehead and into her large black eyes.

Finally, having tightly covered her face, with only her eyes visible, she said, "There is nobody at home, please come later."

"But you are here," the stranger insisted and went on. "I have come from the government and we are doing a survey. We have come to know that there are no newborn girls in this village and we are going house to house to find out why this is so."

"Please come back later." she said as she shut the door in his face, blushing profusely.

The next morning, the stranger came again.

This time, her father and brothers were at home. They answered all his queries as he filled out some forms. He looked up and smiled in acknowledgement of her presence, when, with lowered eyes, she came to serve him fresh milk, her head and face covered again, only her eyes visible.

"What was it that attracted her to him?" she wondered later as she lay on some hay beside the cows that hot afternoon. She finally had some time away from her household chores and she thought about him.

He was kind and gentle, so much unlike the men in her family who treated her no better than the cows they kept. She had no voice, could not have any dreams, and had been taught since childhood that she could never compare herself with her brothers. She was worked like a slave, fed little and treated like a liability which the parents wished to get rid of as soon as possible.

The stranger had actually noticed her and even considered her worthy to answer some questions. She had seen it all on the small television in front of which her father and brothers usually languished in the evenings, while she was only allowed to steal glimpses at it. Girls were going to school and colleges. They were working. They were also reading the news. She had seen movies and how she envied the dresses and the make-up they wore. They could smile and even laugh loudly and move around freely with men. And here she was, always having to cover her face, including her lovely smile and work like a slave in her own house.

Veena was all of 17–years-old.

A week later, the stranger crossed her path again when she had gone to fetch water from the village well. Greeting her, he again smiled at her. Veena felt a strong pull towards him and could not but help and smile back at him.

This time, she was sure her heart did a somersault. It beat so loudly she felt like those around her could also hear its beating.

She had done the unthinkable. She ran back home as fast as her legs could carry her. She had actually allowed her veil to slip and exchanged a smile with this man.

And from that day onward began the coy exchange of smiles. Every day, he would meet her when she went to fetch water. Sometimes, he would slowly follow her. At other times, he would whistle at her and, still other times, he would just watch her as she chatted with the other girls at the well, acutely conscious of his constant and loving gaze at her.

Veena felt betrayed by her own body and she began to return his advances.

He belonged to another caste and another religion, she soon found out from him. He had never been married and had recently been transferred to the local village government school. All these details were of no consequence anyway because they were both very much in love. They began to meet quietly under the shady trees. Their clandestine meetings did not go unnoticed. In the small village and with an even smaller populace, there was always someone walking through the fields or some prying old woman keeping a watch or if nobody else, a little boy minding the cows as they met and word reached Veena's father.

"How dare you? That's why I wanted her to be married as early as possible. It is the Chinese food and the television that are ruining our girls.

"I should not have listened to you and married her off in childhood," her father roared to the mother.

Her elder brother gave her one blow and off she went

reeling on the ground. Two more blows and she was pulled over to give company to the cows that she milked each morning and evening.

"Now, it is your responsibility to see that she does not leave the house," her father added, "or I will behead both of you," as the mother and daughter each quivered like a leaf.

The mother, terrified herself, tried to comfort Veena, "This is our fate. We cannot make our own choice. Don't you even think of marrying someone for love. There will be corpses all around. Do you want bloodshed?"

Barely able to speak, Veena watched the cows, as through their long lashes they looked down on her. "Am I any different from them? A cow is what I am, nothing more."

Dirt from the beaten earth floor clung to her lacerated flesh. By the time her mother was allowed to tend to her, the wounds had become infected and a high fever seized her.

A few days later, Veena succumbed to her injuries.

To make an example for the other village girls, her corpse was hung on the tree in the center of the village.

~ 17 ~

LIVING A LIE

"The fault is not in our stars, but in ourselves."
-Shakespeare

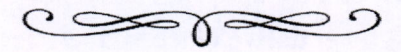

As I cycled around the large campus where we lived when I was a child, accompanied by my friends, I often saw her. She had thick black hair, spread out on her back to dry, with a large red bindi (dot on forehead) and her center parting filled with red powder (a mark of being married). She carried a large puja thali (worship tray) in her hand and she was accompanied by the housemaid, who demurely followed her everywhere, from the market to the temple. Her husband was a tailor. A mismatch, I had often heard my mother say, for Pawa had been well advanced in age when she met this man. Knowing she would not get a suitable match and being under pressure in the conservative society, she had settled for the tailor. At least he had a steady job and she had a good job as well as the accommodation.

The fact that she was well advanced in age meant that she would not have any children of her own.

From time to time, the servant would change. As a child, I had no way of knowing why this was, until the time I grew up and heard the story from my mother.

The tailor husband was a womanizer. Threatening to walk out on her, Pawa relented by letting her husband sleep with the maids from time to time. Once in a while, the maid would not comply and would run out of the house. This meant the neighbors would know about the arrangement and this is something Pawa was not willing to risk. After all, she had a position and a reputation to hold on to.

So, on her husband's threats, Pawa brought a poor orphan girl from her native place and left her at the husband's mercy.

Time passed and Pawa began to say that she was the younger sister whose husband is in another town. Soon the "sister" became pregnant and had two boys.

The sister also began to put a red bindi (dot on forehead) and filled her hair center parting (symbols of being married and accompanied Pawa to the temple.

Pawa worked outside the home and the "sister" worked inside the home. It was a happy looking joint family. The tailor husband kick-started his scooter every morning to go to work with a smug smile on his face, and why not?

He had not one, but two women to serve him and nobody dare say a word to him.

They all lived a lie.

~ 18 ~

"I Slipped"

"Violence against women is a manifestation of historically unequal power relations between men and women, which has led to domination over and discrimination against women by men and to the prevention of the full advancement of women," according to the United Nations Declaration on the Elimination of Violence against Women, General Assembly Resolution, December 1993.

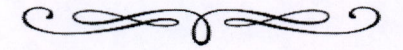

Kajol was getting ready for the hospital. It was her night shift. She worked in the laboratory of a large hospital in Delhi.

Her complexion was rosy and dark eyes adorned her pretty face. She loved to dress up and wear make-up which further accentuated her beauty. Her slim figure belied the fact that she was a mother of two little children.

And then her husband came from work, drunk as usual.

"Are you going to work or to meet your boyfriend at the hospital?" he asked.

"Don't talk rubbish. I have fed the kids and put them to bed. There is hot food on the stove for you. I am running late for work. See you in the morning." Kajol brushed past him not wishing to engage herself when he was drunk and she was late for her duty anyway.

And that is when he hit her.

"How dare you speak to me like this," he yelled, and off she went, banging her head against the wall and breaking her ribs.

"I slipped in the bathroom while getting ready to come to work," she confided in me as I accompanied my husband on his hospital visits.

Head injury and ribs broken, Kajol was to be confined to her bed for the next few weeks and was yet smiling bravely and protecting her husband.

I looked at her with my prying eyes asking her a question. I was not going to believe her story. She evaded my eyes.

Her husband was good looking and tall. He had a stable job and was a devout father and husband, or that is what I had been led to believe by none other than Kajol herself.

But inside the home, he was the devil incarnate. Jealous of Kajol's good looks and economic independence, he would drink, and often beat her up.

Kajol's brothers were aware of the battering she

received at the hands of her husband. Murderous rage would fill them each time they heard her plight, but they were helpless because Kajol would not allow them to touch her husband.

The worst part was when he would land up drunk in the hospital where she worked. He would fight and shout at her, much to her embarrassment. Her colleagues suggested that she divorce him, but she would not hear of it.

"I have two children. I will bear as long as I can bear. I do not wish to separate or go back to my father's house. Our society blames the woman in such a case. I will be considered an easy prey for one and all," she explained in defense as she desperately tried to hold on to a bad marriage.

Suhail, Kajol's husband, got more and more courageous as time passed. He knew his wife's brothers would not touch him. He had multiple affairs with women, would get drunk at night and the police would call up Kajol to come and take him home. Kajol's brothers began to get weary of her because she would not let them handle him their way.

And here she lay, once again, having been battered and still protecting him. "I should have looked where I was walking," she said again.

Kajol had been raped while she was on a date with her fiancé, now her husband, before their marriage. Taking him to be a respectable man, she had trusted him and he had abused her trust. The timid Kajol continued to be ill-treated by her husband, even after many years of marriage.

"Suhail is at home, looking after the children. I am comfortable here as my colleagues are taking good care of me," she says, trying to hide a tear that escaped her eyes.

After many counseling sessions with the women in the church, Kajol finally opened up. She informed them that Suhail had beaten her up even before they were married. "I have often contemplated suicide but then I look at my young children and choose to suffer silently."

The church women began to pray as the church elders confronted Suhail. "You know, if Kajol reports you to the police, first, they will put you behind bars and then they will speak to you. Be a man and stop hitting women."

With the cat out of the bag, Suhail is now held accountable by the local church leadership and Kajol has people to pray for her.

~ 19 ~

WOMB FOR RENT

"Snowflakes are one of nature's most fragile things, but just look at what they can do when they stick together."
-Vesta M. Kelly

Meera awoke sweating profusely with her heart palpitating. She looked at the clock on the wall. It was 2 a.m. Once again, the same nightmare woke her up.

She had been having the recurrent nightmare since she had parted with her son. She could hear the baby cry and see herself reach out to him but she could not touch him. He was too far away for her to reach out to lift and hug. Meera began to weep again.

Hailing from Gujarat, the tall, fair and big-boned Meera had been married to an alcoholic at an early age.

Having fallen on bad times, with two girl children to

support, Meera had no option but to fend for herself.

She was determined that she would educate her daughters. "I want them to receive an education and training so that they can live a life of dignity and be independent financially."

However, there was little that she could do. Meera trudged along life's journey as her children went to a local government school where education and mid-day meal were provided free of charge, as were the school uniforms.

And then one day, a neighbor told her about "surrogate motherhood", meaning that a woman would bear the child of another couple in her womb for nine months and after delivery, hand over the child to the parents. If Meera became a surrogate mother, it would fetch her a lot of money. Of course, she would have to stay away from her family for nine months.

Meera had never heard of such a thing before. How could she bear another man's child without having a physical relationship?

"Why don't you go and see this doctor who is looking for tall and fair women like you. She will explain everything to you. You have already borne two children and had no complications. The doctor will inject you and you will become pregnant. It will be their child, not yours. Just like some poor people in our country have to donate blood and kidneys for money, you can rent out your womb. Just make sure that you do not become emotionally attached to the child."

Meera could hardly believe what she was hearing.

On one side was the fact that after keeping the child in her womb for nine months, she would have to hand over the child. Would the child not be in her body? Would she not grow him with her blood? How then, would she part with the child?

As all of these questions haunted her, she saw her girls growing into maturity and the thought of what would happen to them if she did not decide soon, forced her into visiting the doctor.

Meera's alcoholic husband was more than pleased to hear of this proposal and readily agreed to release her. "It is only a matter of nine months and you are not sleeping with another man. It will be a little medical procedure." He pushed Meera as she wondered about the dangers of playing with nature. "It will be my child that I raise in my womb. Then why do I have to give him away. I will feel as if I am selling my child."

"But imagine the good money we will get. Our poverty will be a thing of the past. We can build a house. Our daughters can marry well."

Meera talked herself into surrogacy and was whisked off to Mumbai for nine months. There were other women in the nursing home with her. They were very well looked after. They had all the good food, tonics, rest and entertainment provided to them. Meera had never had it this good her entire life. "Just do not attach yourself to the baby. It belongs to someone else. You will not even be told whether you gave birth to a boy or a girl. That is the contract you have signed," she was told.

Meera came home with a lot of money in her hand but also with a brooding sense of remorse. Depression and nightmares became routine and she felt guilty.

Deep inside, Meera knew that something was not right. She missed the child she bore and often cried herself to sleep. And it was on one of those nights that sleep eluded her, that she heard a radio program called *"Khush Khabri"* in which they were giving information on renting the womb and telling of all the dangers relating to it.

But then, in India, to be a woman and to be poor is the worst crime. Meera could not believe it. She had never heard such a broadcast on FM radio before. She drank in all the information and then decided to no longer use her body like this. Instead, she joined the village self-help group of women to earn a living for herself and her children. "I will not put myself in further agony," she decided, wondering if God will forgive her for what she had done by renting out her womb for other people.

~ 20 ~

FIRED

*"Life is like a boxing ring.
Defeat is not declared if you fall, it is
declared when you refuse to get up."*
                    -Anonymous

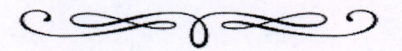

The news had spread like wild fire. Leela Nair, the first woman CEO of a well-known multi-national corporation based in Delhi had just been fired. No allegations had been leveled against her. She had just been informed to step out of her role and that it had been a decision of the board of directors.

Leela, fair, broad-shouldered and 5-foot-6 in her heels, with a tight bun on her nape and large brown, intelligent eyes was single at 45. Having been so busy focusing on her career, she had never really found the time for romance and marriage.

Leela is among the very few who have broken the glass

ceiling and reached the top position in spite of her gender.

This is her story.

"The horror of that night continues to haunt me, no matter how many years have elapsed since the day I was publicly stripped of my dignity and left to bleed and die, broken and bruised by the people who had worked alongside with me for 20-odd years.

It was November, the onset of winter. It was past 10:30 p.m. and I was sitting in my office. This was nothing unusual, as I often worked late nights because there was so much to be done.

But tonight was altogether different.

I was sitting and waiting to be summoned for the Board meeting that had begun at 9 a.m that morning. I was not totally unaware. I knew something was amiss when soon after I had started the meeting, I was requested to leave for a time of executive session of the Board.

As I waited with my team, or what I thought was my team, keeping full distance with me, memories of 20 years gone by filled my mind, one by one.

My life with this organization had been one painful episode after another. Working with a maverick boss who liked to see the women staff serve him, he tolerated me because I was good with my work. It had not been easy. When asked by the Board to hand over the reins of the organization to me so he could retire, he threw the file on the floor saying, "I will never hand over this organization to a woman."

Tantrums aside, he had to do it because the organization was sinking and a change of guard was a necessity to set the house in order.

My appointment to replace him had left the Board shell shocked because it was the decision of the international office which wanted to make a new beginning with good financial practices and transparency as the main objective. My diplomatic and negotiating skills, which added to my already good international and local networking, was found to be very suitable for a time such as that. And at the age of 39, I was appointed the CEO of this multi-national corporation.

I had sensed resistance from day one of my taking office, an undercurrent of resentment in the men who served with me on the team. After all, I had replaced an elderly man who was known for his maverick ways of operating. With his dictatorial attitude and street-smart ways, he believed in throwing money around and purchasing people. With a loud booming voice, people shivered with fear every time he walked into the office building. The staff had become so used to being kicked around by him that no one minded as long as he threw money at them or left loopholes for them to help themselves even as he helped himself.

The first year was shaky and I found little cooperation. But as I began to travel around and patiently connect with the staff, the ice breaking began. Things began to look up with regard to the image of the company and having worked with international partners over the years, I already had their goodwill.

Further, found to be doing well with my cost-effective measures in the face of economic recession, blocking loopholes and introducing best financial practices, the Board had decided to give me a three-year extension. After that extension was up, they were so happy that they gave me a bonus and extended it to five years with an appreciation bonus. A knock on my door drew me out of my thoughts as I had been finally summoned to the Board room. I looked at my watch. It was 10:30 p.m. I wondered what took them so long when they had begun the meeting at 9 a.m that day.

Before the full Board, the woman chairperson addressed me, asking me to step out of the CEO position.

No explanations were offered.

No consolation.

No words of advice.

And why did I even expect this?

Most of the male Board members and my male team members had stay home wives who supported their husbands and ate after their husbands had finished eating.

I had expected the woman chairperson to stand up for me. But she chose to ride along with the current. A day earlier, she had confided in me saying, "All I can see here is that they cannot handle a woman CEO."

I was calm. I smiled and looked at each Board member in the eyes and also caught the wicked smiles and dancing eyes of my male and female teammates.

As I understood later, some senior male staff rallied some unhappy staff together to write against me to the international office, which believed them. As for the puppet Indian Board, it bowed under the international pressure.

The typical Indian way says that what a woman thinks or speaks is inconsequential because women in India are the second sex.

"Were you surprised with what happened?" is a question I am often asked.

"No, not at all. When the international office had asked me to take on the CEO position at a critical time, I had asked them to get an Indian man. This was expected."

"Why didn't you go to court?" I am further asked.

"I had worked so hard to grow the organization and did not have the heart to bring it down. I just chose to move on."

One prominent government minister had remarked at a public meeting, "We are a democracy and even the worst of criminals with all the evidences in place is given a fair trial."

"Fair trial! What's that? Remember, I am an Indian woman." says Leela

Leela had a choice; either indulge herself in self-pity or go out of her home, look at the hurting and wounded women and help them. She chose the latter and founded a non-profit organization which encourages women and helps them to bravely carry on with their lives.

~ 21 ~

"I Feel Dirty"

*"If someone dreams alone, then it remains
only a dream. If many dream together,
then this is the beginning of a new reality."*
— Anonymous

The warden of the Christian hostel was having a tough time. It was holiday time from school and while many girls looked forward to leaving school and spending time with their families, Shabana was not too keen. These girls either had a single mother, an elderly grandmother, an ailing grandfather, an aunt or a guardian, but they did have someone. Most of these families could not afford to look after the girls because of their low economic status. Moreover, the kidnapping of little girls had risen to an alarming high and it was too dangerous to leave the young girls alone in the slum, unattended and at the mercy of a trafficker or a rapist. According to official reports, two out of three children trafficked are girls and in such a given condition, a Christian hostel in Delhi run by the church is a safe haven for them.

All the girls were leaving on the last day of school, except Shabana. In spite of the official announcement given, her mother did not come nor respond to the phone calls.

Shabana, all of 8-years-old, is a fair child with large, light brown eyes that sometimes forget to bat as she intensely gazes into my face. With light brown hair cut short, her lips curve into a pretty smile.

"Her mother does not wish to take her, not even for a few days," said the warden to me.

"But why is that?" I asked and then the story spilled out.

Shabana's mother is a sex worker. With no means of a livelihood after the death of her husband, who left her with young Shabana, a well-meaning neighbor from their remote village in Uttar Pradesh offered this young widow a job in the big city.

Unfortunately, she hailed from a family that had tutored her, saying, "Once you are married, do not look back. We are dead to you. You have to fend for yourself. No coming back."

It was her bad luck that she became a widow and nobody wanted any part of her. Lonely and desolate, the neighbor had come to her like a Messiah. He had a good job in Delhi and took good care of his wife and children. He had heard about her plight and offered to help.

"Come with me. You will have a great job and your daughter will also be looked after well. This is a place where the madam allows you to bring your baby with you."

And so she agreed and bid goodbye to her village.

All of 23-years-old, Shabana's mother came to Delhi and was tricked into flesh trade. For the sake of feeding herself, with no possible route of escape and nobody to help her, Shabana's mother surrendered to serving an endless stream of men who were sent to her day and night.

There were many other women like her in the brothel. They had young children, too, and a good woman looked after the children while they worked. Nevertheless, she wanted Shabana to stay away from this place – it was dirty and toxic. She was horrified when the brothel keepers looked at her 5-year-old, saying, "She is the spitting image of you. We will get her started early. She will fetch a good price and then you can rest."

"That, I will never allow! I'd rather throttle her with my own hands. This is a living hell," she would say to herself and pray, not sure if anybody was listening. She had lost faith in God and people alike. Life in their world included street fights, physical abuse, horrible language, prostitution, lying, stabbing, even murder.

And then one day she heard about a Christian girls' hostel in the big city. This was where young Shabana was brought, to a refuge which became her home and where she would be looked after, fed, educated and cared for.

"I feel dirty when I come to visit my daughter and she tells me about all the good things she is learning. I am grateful she is safe and looked after but as she is growing up, I cannot look into her eyes," she told the warden.

"I will visit her, but I do not wish to take her to where I live. Please let her live in the hostel during school holidays. I have no place to take her," she pleaded with the warden.

"Also, please help me as I wish to make a new beginning. I wish for my daughter to be proud of me when she grows up."

~ 22 ~

ABANDONED

*"In three words I can sum up everything
I've learned about life, it goes on."*
-Robert Frost

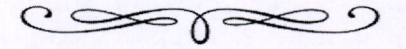

"Every single day I leave the house, either I go to visit my daughter, my sister, a friend or to some religious gathering. The problem is my daughter-in-law; she hates me. I have only one son and one daughter. I come from a family of three girls, so I had so much looked forward to having a son. I love him very much. He was a good boy until he got married. Soon after the birth of his own two sons, his wife began to torture me. I have a reasonably good house, which my husband left in my name. We all live comfortably, but for petty reasons my daughter-in-law picks on me and fights with me. I am going to be 70-years-old and cannot handle all the shouting and fighting. One day, my son came to me and said, "Please write this house in my name or my wife will leave me and go."

"After I die, you will get it and then I wish to divide it between your sister and you." I told him.

"If you do that, my wife will leave me and also take the children with her."

I gave in to his emotional blackmail and signed the legal papers he put before me.

I thought now I can rest in peace, but ever since I signed, my daughter-in-law has become worse.

Now she says this is her house and that I have to leave.

"But don't you know there are laws protecting the interests of senior citizens? You just need to go to the police station," my friends insist.

"But what is the point?" I counter.

"If I take legal help, my son will never see my face again. After all, he has to light my funeral pyre. How else will I attain salvation? This is all because of my karma. It is my destiny and I will continue to suffer. At least because of the fear of my daughter, my son has not left me in the *kumbh mela* (a religious gathering of Hindus who go to dip themselves in the River Ganges) where thousands of widows are left every year, abandoned and destitute.

"I am happy that I can at least see his face daily and also the faces of my grandsons who love me very much."

(Mrs. Goel's story as told to the author)

INTERVENTION OF DISHA FOUNDATION
www.dishafoundationindia.in

*"When the going gets tough,
the tough get going."*
-Joseph P. Kennedy

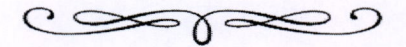

Our weekly Hindi broadcasts called *"Khush Khabri"* (meaning good news) through All-India Radio's national FM station is estimated to reach 80 million people and advocates against sex-selective abortions and strives to change the Indian mind-set so that the birth of a girl is no longer considered bad news.

We advocate against abortion, sex-selective abortions, gender disparity, child marriage, domestic violence, suicide, honor killing, dowry, surrogacy, rapes, and we promote the Christian world view on these issues.

We also promote gender equality, inculcating of values within the family, encouraging the authority of the father, and the influence of the mother to shape values of the new generation. We encourage women to get educated, become self-reliant and have the courage to dream big.

We create awareness about the laws and give medical knowledge pertaining to health issues.

Our weekly Hindi broadcasts, "Baat Pate ki" create awareness against trafficking, hoping to reach the vulnerable children before the traffickers do and thus arrest trafficking, "Baat pate ki" (meaning subject of importance).

Our weekly broadcasts in Bengali *"Ashar Aalo"* also create awareness against trafficking.

We also provide the following :
- Financial support for education of girls through school and college
- Vocational skills to girls / women and economically weak
- Employment opportunities
- Micro-finance for small business run by women
- Financial support for Mid- day meals for street children
- Financial support the economically weak and abandoned elderly
- Expertise in organizing conferences for Christians to create awareness and encourage them to prayerfully engage with their context
- Expertise in organizing workshops/ seminars with school/ college students with the goal of moulding their minds towards gender- equality and women empowerment

ABOUT THE AUTHOR

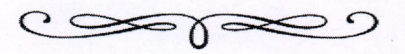

Vinita Shaw was born in New Delhi, India. A journalist, she has many published articles to her credit, including a book written in English called, "I Heard a Voice," which has been translated into Finnish language and some portions into Dutch language. A collection of short stories, the book is a testimony to the power of radio in India.

The first woman CEO of Trans World Radio-India, Vinita has 20 years of experience in radio and print journalism. She serves on the International Council of World Evangelical Alliance and the Board of Evangelical Fellowship of India.

She also serves as a Consultant to international donor bodies who wish to serve in India.

Vinita is the Founder/CEO of Disha Foundation, a non-profit organization in India. Vinita is a strong advocate of women and children and speaks to the Indian masses on All India Radio (AIR) national FM channel through her weekly broadcasts asking them to come out of their centuries old mindset and walk in the light.

Married to Pastor Timothy Shaw of the Diocese of Delhi, Church of North India, for 22 years, they have two children and live in New Delhi, India.